LITTLE BIOGRAPHIES OF BIG PEOPLE

BEETHOVEN

By Joan Stoltman

Gareth Stevens PUBLISHING

Please visit our website, www.garethstevens.com. For a free color catalog of all our high-quality books, call toll free 1-800-542-2595 or fax 1-877-542-2596.

Library of Congress Cataloging-in-Publication Data

Names: Stoltman, Joan, author.
Title: Beethoven / Joan Stoltman.
Description: New York : Gareth Stevens Publishing, [2019] | Series: Little biographies of big people | Includes index.
Identifiers: LCCN 2018014469| ISBN 9781538228920 (library bound) | ISBN 9781538232156 (pbk.) | ISBN 9781538232163 (6 pack)
Subjects: LCSH: Beethoven, Ludwig van, 1770-1827–Juvenile literature. | Composers–Austria–Biography–Juvenile literature.
Classification: LCC ML3930.B4 S76 2019 | DDC 780.92 [B] –dc23
LC record available at https://lccn.loc.gov/2018014469

Published in 2019 by
Gareth Stevens Publishing
111 East 14th Street, Suite 349
New York, NY 10003

Designer: Tanya Dellaccio
Editor: Kate Mikoley

Photo credits: series art Yulia Glam/Shutterstock.com; cover UniversalImagesGroup/Getty Images; p. 5 https://commons.wikimedia.org/wiki/File:Thirteen-year-old_Beethoven.jpg; p. 7 Imagno/Hulton Archive/Getty Images; p. 9 Imagno/Hulton Fine Art Collection/Getty Images; pp. 11, 21 DEA/A. DAGLI ORTI/De Agostini/Getty Images; p. 13 Hulton Archive/Getty Images; p. 15 Three Lions/Hulton Archive/Getty Images; p. 17 Heritage Images/Hulton Archive/Getty Images; p. 19 Rischgitz/Hulton Archive/Getty Images.

Printed in the United States of America

CPSIA compliance information: Batch #CW19GS: For further information contact Gareth Stevens, New York, New York at 1-800-542-2595.

CONTENTS

A Star Is Born! 4
Tough Childhood 6
Composing Begins. 10
Working Hard 12
Vienna 14
Is It Over? 16
Making Great Music 18
Thanks, Beethoven! 20
Glossary. 22
For More Information. 23
Index 24

Boldface words appear in the glossary.

A Star Is Born!

Ludwig van Beethoven was born in 1770 in Bonn, a city in what is now Germany. He was one of seven children, but only three lived to be adults. Beethoven was named after his grandfather who was a famous **musician**.

Tough Childhood

As a child, Beethoven was a talented piano player. His father wanted him to be a famous child musician. He made Beethoven practice for hours. Beethoven learned several **instruments**, but he was **punished** for making even tiny mistakes. He started playing in front of people at age 7!

After Beethoven's grandfather died, his family began having money troubles. Beethoven stopped going to school around age 11, but he kept studying music. He learned from the court **organ** player in Bonn. He began learning how to compose, or write music.

BEETHOVEN'S GRANDFATHER

Composing Begins

By age 12, Beethoven had composed his first piece of music! In 1787, he was sent to Vienna, Austria, the center of the music world. He was supposed to study with the famous composer Mozart. However, Beethoven's mother got very sick. He had to return home.

Working Hard

Back in Bonn, Beethoven kept playing music and also began to teach it. He met many important people through his music. In 1792, Beethoven returned to Vienna, where he soon became known as the one of the best piano players. People cried when he played.

Vienna

Beethoven studied with several musicians in Vienna. He began to work more on composing music. Beethoven soon became more famous for his composing than he was for playing the piano. Beethoven's life appeared to be going well.

Is It Over?

Beethoven had begun going **deaf** around age 25. He didn't think he could live without hearing. But he knew he still had a lot of music left to write. Beethoven often took long walks, writing his ideas for music in notebooks.

"What I have in my heart must come out; that is the reason why I compose."

—Beethoven

Making Great Music

Before Beethoven, many composers thought **melodies** were for singing. But Beethoven wrote melodies for instruments. His music was also very emotional, or full of feelings. He composed some of his greatest works after he had already gone deaf.

Thanks, Beethoven!

When Beethoven died at age 56, around 20,000 people came out to honor him. We still honor him today as one of the greatest composers who has ever lived. Beethoven played a part in making music more than just something that sounded nice. It became an important art!

GLOSSARY

deaf: not able to hear

instrument: an object used to make music

melody: a pleasing series of musical notes that form the main part of a song or piece of music

musician: one who plays, makes, or sings music

organ: a musical instrument that has a keyboard and pipes of different lengths and makes sound by pushing air through the pipes

punish: to make someone suffer for wrongdoing

FOR MORE INFORMATION

BOOKS

Celenza, Anna Harwell. *Beethoven's Heroic Symphony*. Watertown, MA: Charlesbridge, 2016.

Mattern, Joanne. *Ludwig van Beethoven: A Revolutionary Composer*. New York, NY: Children's Press, 2017.

Venezia, Mike. *Ludwig van Beethoven*. New York, NY: Children's Press, 2017

WEBSITES

Ludwig van Beethoven—A Music Appreciation Lesson for Kids
www.pianolessons4children.com/composers/beethoven.php
Read about Beethoven and then listen to some of his music.

Music for Kids: Famous Pianists
www.ducksters.com/musicforkids/famous_pianists.php
This list has facts about many great musicians, including Beethoven!

Publisher's note to educators and parents: Our editors have carefully reviewed these websites to ensure that they are suitable for students. Many websites change frequently, however, and we cannot guarantee that a site's future contents will continue to meet our high standards of quality and educational value. Be advised that students should be closely supervised whenever they access the internet.

INDEX

Bonn 4, 8, 12

composing 8, 10, 14, 17, 18

deafness 16, 18

family 4, 6, 8, 10

melodies 18

Mozart 10

organ 8

performing 6, 12

piano 6, 12, 14

school 8

teaching 12

Vienna, Austria 10, 12, 14